Mauri Zucchi

Money Management Tips.

In this book we will apply practical theorems of money management, namely the management of risk in the business. This discipline, which is very important for financial survival, embraces almost all businesses. But is it really what you think? We will go to disassemble different theorems, so get ready: a good glass of coffee, wine or tea and we leave.

Money management: overview in general.

Money Management derives from the English "management of one's own capital" and it is therefore easy to understand what it is. Money management (often abbreviated to MM) has always been present in everything we do. We think about when we do the shopping, even without thinking about it, we evaluate the prices of the products according to our needs / portfolio. No one with a shred of brain buys 11 in his pocket 10, right? The same thing is applied to business, work and life. Sometimes we forget about this important activity when we do business, getting losses. Other times, however, we abuse it, not obtaining satisfactory results. So here we must weigh this discipline.

Money Management: how much should I risk?

Always in the MM manuals we find information in which they tell us to "risk little", but this is not always the case. Take for example a good restaurant. To open it, we need several capitals, we make 500,000 usd. The company that created it established that it will take 5 years to repay these expenses. 5 years net profit equal to zero. What will the sixth year happen? The expenses will decrease dramatically and finally there will be profits to be divided among the members. However, there is always the risk that something could happen in those 5 years of expenses, perhaps a natural disaster, or a major crisis or whatever. The company should in this case, add more capital and postpone net profit for a few years. But let's go back to the initial example. Under normal conditions, that restaurant, after 5 years, will have net profits of around 100,000 usd per year, and therefore a return on investment (ROI) of 100% after 10 years in total.

If it was you, with that restaurant, you probably would have made a "suicide" venture, spending 500.000usd on the nail. But the company has a money management behind several million usd, useful to deal with risk. And here comes the first point. Money generates money, but it always depends on your availability.

Let's take a more humane case. Yourself. You have 100,000 usd in the bank. Only those. Would you invest the whole sum in an activity? Mind you might be a good business that can generate a salary. But the risk of ending up under a bridge is high. Because you have only one shot in the barrel. By dividing the sum into more business instead, in theory, you will have more possibilities. Provided that they are not business useless.

Business: quality or quantity?

The question is the following: better so many business or just one, if you have a sum? The answer is always the same: it depends. It depends on the type of business and the context. Let's take an example. Clara has 50,000 usd, and is undecided between 2 roads: invest all in a share of a bar started, or open two or three small activities not too demanding (two small creperie, plus an online job). What to do?

In this case, it is better to invest everything in the first context. We explain why. A bar started is synonymous with constant revenue (which is to be established through the members, and from here will set the price for the quota), if then the share is important, after having evaded any cheats, it is clear that the revenue will be adequate. Starting from zero in two creperies, at least not having experience and luck of location, it could be a hole in the water. Investing 20.000usd in a pancake house can not therefore make us think about earning huge sums, and almost all similar activities are in the same situation. Therefore, there would be a stalemate / loss by choosing the second option, even if diversified investments.

Diversifying modest or shoddy businesses does not always lead to returns. We need to focus on quality, always and in any case. If you do not find anything, do not invest, rather than diversify between business useless!

Money Management Financial: basic rules.

The MM being an effective discipline to control their money, is effectively used in online trading, one of the most difficult jobs ever. As we know, markets are subject to hundreds of variables every day, which is why a good expense containment strategy can help us. We will see in this paragraph how to operate.

- **1. Commissions.** Choosing a broker offers the right tools for us is a primary concern, but in addition to this we look for a broker with the lowest possible fees. Of course it must be certified and solid.
- **2. Leverage.** Leverage is important but not for money management. Rather than leveraging, you need to learn how to convert stoploss into cash. A stoploss is not made up of points or percentages, but of money. If I have a 1000usd account and use trade limits of around 10usd, those are my stops. The placement of such will occur accordingly with this information. It is also possible to divide it into several trades, in order to have my total stop always around 10-15 usd for that pattern or graphic. Leverage therefore only relies on certain instruments, for example buying a lot on usd / rub is

not the same lever that buy it on eur / usd. The first requires much more. Here this is the only problem of the lever. But as far as money management is concerned, it has nothing to do with it. You can also use 100% leverage if our trade is very short, with tight stops, and respects the 10usd stop as in the example. Leverage therefore has nothing to do with money management.

• **Quality**. And here we come back to the previous paragraph about diversification with creperies. They have always taught us to use a positive risk-profit, that is the second major of the first, but is it always like that?

The quality in trading.

Use a positive risk-profit, or the second major of the first: but is it always like that?
No, in many cases, the most delicious ones, it's not like that. Take for example a multiday trader, who uses tight stops of 10 points and profit target of 50.

The market, as we know, is a crazy spinning top, then a strict stop, statistically, as in this example, doing trades without really useful information, in the best case we will return a 4 trades equal and a winning, not making us earn anything.

In this example it is clear that, despite having adequate money management, and an excellent risk-profit ratio (1: 5), we find ourselves losers! Let's now look at an example with a negative profit risk (1: 3), but that brings profit.

We have identified a stock of shares that always move in the same range, but not always. It happens that every ten trades, the price deviates a lot from the channel. Our profit target will therefore be short (1), while our stoploss will be positioned outside the price context to avoid strange movements of this (stoploss = 3 times the tp). Now if in general, over the years we have had 9 positive and 1 negative trades using this system, here the trading system allows us to use a negative risk-profit ratio, but to be profitable!

This is just an example, but as we have seen, it is not at all true that a profit risk in favor of the latter is mandatory. On the other hand, even a car salesman has a negative risk-profit ratio. Often buy vintage cars to exhibit and resell at a price slightly higher than purchased (stoploss = car price). With all the risk of being robbed or having damage to the car.

So here in the trading, rather than the management of the risk (which still remains important) the quality of the trade is necessary. If a trade gives me a 90% profit I can also decide to insert a stop much wider than the possible gain (attention, the stoploss must always be present!). The risk-profit ratio depends on the quality of the trade: the higher and more accurate, the more I can afford a wide stoploss. In any case, in online trading, one must always remain an escape route, even with "certain" data. Let's see why.

Trading without stoploss.

Nassim Taleb is a market researcher, mathematician, who has written several risk management manuals. In short, it states that each market is subject to a "black swan", or an "x" moment in which you will lose all your money.

This factor is rare, but constant. In fact, if we check some dates, we will notice that he is right. In 2001, with the collapse of the twin towers, millions of trading accounts were burned. The same in 2008 with the US banking crisis. the same in 2015 with the Swiss franc. All these events, they would have perhaps put a piece in many trading accounts, using a stoploss.

The stoploss is nothing more than a machine order, so its execution depends on your broker / supplier of liquidity. In abnormal situations, it is not always possible to control it. The fact remains that an inserted stoploss is still almost always a guarantee, even at a legal level. Do not insert a stoploss is therefore, in the long run, a big problem.

In 90% of cases a stoploss is performed, good or bad, at the price you requested. In anomalous situations, it can be performed with a discrepancy of a few points. In even more anomalous situations, which occur rarely, it could also be performed at 100 points of difference. It is clear that using a high lever in these conditions is swept away, but it is also true that a high leverage involves a very tight stop that is closed instantly, before many others. The fact remains that using high leverage is only for experienced traders who take advantage of certain market conditions, inefficiencies, and so on. To be discouraged for intermediate traders / novices.

So back to the stoploss, always insert it. If you do not like the "spinning" movement of the market or if you believe stop hunting (stop hunting), try to insert it away from the price, but always put it.

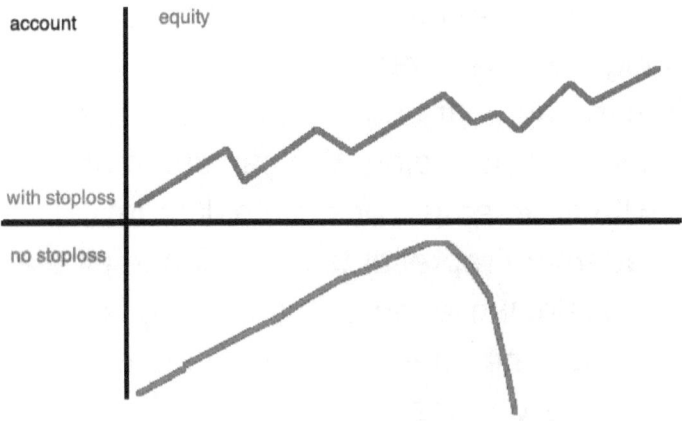

account | equity

with stoploss

no stoploss

Image above: the green account has the stoploss, and defends itself against possible rarely occurring catastrophes. Account 2 in red does not use stoploss, it always gains until it is catastrophic. Losing everything.

Money management: practice.

We have reached the paragraph of the practice, very important for trading. We will then move on to how to try and increase this account. In fact, if money management is used to defend ourselves, it also requires the right strategy to increase the bill, which is called Compounding. We can summarize everything with an example of a football team: money management represents the defense plus a part of the midfield, while the Compounding is nothing more than the attack and the offensive part of the midfield, the one that must make points to increase the Ranking. But now let's go back to the "defensive" practical part, always part of money management.

Managing your account: differences between mini-account and large-account.

Surviving in trading is sacrosanct, but does an account with 1.000usd make sense compared to one from 100.000usd, if both generate the same risks and percentages of profit?

We try to understand one thing. Profits have a percentage. Let's say that our trading system generate 2% per month. On our 100,000usd account this will be excellent: we get a salary, with a fairly low risk. But now we come to the small account, the one from 1.000usd. He, too, with the same trading system, generates 2% monthly with a low risk. But does it make sense to generate 2% monthly on this account? Let's talk about 20usd monthly!

Here, then, that the mini-bill must be adequate to dare more, obviously obtaining greater risks. The 100.000usd account, on the other hand, must be treated with gloves, at least if your availability is not millionaire. In general, the bigger the account, the more risk and profits must be contained. The reason is simple. Losing 1000usd is a negligible fact for almost the entire population on earth, or at least those who trade online. The profits generated by this account are ridiculous and useless. Only by daring (in a reasonable way) a little more and using an aggressive initial Compounding, one has the possibility to take this account to more profitable figures.

Forex money management trading scheme:

account	average stoploss	example of size trade:	risk per day (in %) max all trades
1000usd	>10usd	1000usd 1 microlot per pair	4-6% max
100.000usd	< 1000 usd	0,5 lot per pair 50.000usd	1-2% max

Let's see in detail. 1000usd account: has an average stoploss of 10usd (indicative), but which can be increased up to 50-60 usd (all open trades).

Typically, every trades has a magnitude of 1000usd (leverage 1: 1) or 1 microlot.

10.000usd account: has a smaller stoploss than the smaller account, in total among all open trades it does not reach 2%. In these conditions it uses an even lower lever, so on average 5 minilotti (or half lot) of trade size.

All values are average, and depend on the characteristics of your trading system. In general, the more the trades are large, the lower the buying magnitudes will be.

The more the bill increases in value, the more it will have to be adjusted, and in general the risk will be reduced. This is if we want to make a form of Compounding (increase in account) that we will see later. For the moment we need to know the table above.

Salary account or "explosive" account?

There is a difference between the two accounts. Let's see what it is. A salary account is an account, presumed after having obtained a good strategy, which allows us to live and withdraw money, without this changing its size. Let's take an example. We have an account of 30.000usd that fortunately, every few months, generates us from 3 to 5000usd. When this happens, we take all the money and use it as a salary. Our account remains at 30.000usd. This is an account-salary.

An account that does not require mandatory withdrawals is generally defined as a test account. These very small accounts are used in trading to test strategies with greater risks. The test accounts are more forced to risk, but this does not mean that they are to be thrown away, on the contrary. As the bill increases, you will have to lower the risks, just like the 100,000usd account in the previous paragraph. What changes with respect to the salary account is that it is generally not taken, or only the initial capital can be withdrawn, once a fair amount has been obtained.

The salary-account aims to have a good capital and never go further with money management (it always uses the same dimensions as the trades). The test account adjusts the size of the trades as the account increases. If the trading technique is having a favorable period, the bill will "explode" towards considerable gains. The fact remains that sooner or later a period of stalemate or loss will come, so it is essential, as the account increases, to contain money management and make it less aggressive.

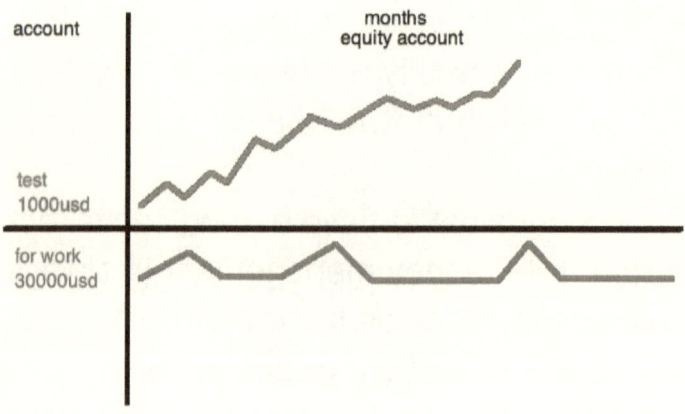

account   months
equity account

test
1000usd

for work
30000usd

In the photo above: salary account (green) and test account (red). The red account has higher earning percentages, but also higher risks. The green account only aims to make profits to be withdrawn from time to time.

I have a small account. What to do?

If you have only one 1000usd account and would like to "live trading", the venture is quite difficult. The road to follow is only one, that is a cross between the test account and the salary account. Given that pulling out a salary from an account of 1000usd, is equivalent to making 80-100% per month of ROI (virtually impossible, except to find inefficiencies of markets), we can instead concentrate on bringing the bill, risking something more like in table above, and then stop increasing the account and use it as a salary account, or with leverage and stop. In this way, transforming the "test" account into the "salary" account brings a leveling of the drawdowns, with a consequent reduction in risks.

Negative periods.

In trading as in any business focused on statistics and mathematics, unfavorable periods may appear concatenated with each other, in this case, sequences of negative trades greater than the positive ones. These occur when a trading system no longer works. The factors can be many, and often, depend only on the market that has changed. In these situations it is advisable to stop and contemplate the markets, especially in the past. Has this dynamic already happened? Do I have to change the market or method? How long should I wait before resuming my strategy? These are all questions that a trader must ask himself. The negative period is called "drawdown". We do not have to wait for "what steps", rather to contemplate possible ways of going out by looking back at historical charts, and in the meantime, stop betraying. When the market resumes the characteristics of your strategy, you can take back the situation. Otherwise look for other markets. Do not wait for the drawdown to burn 40-50% of your account, because then it becomes almost impossible to recover.

Recover losses in%.

Recovering large losses is very difficult in trading. This is because adjusting the lever after you lose, for example 50%, it will take 100% profits to get back on a par. The table below shows the recoveries.

Percent Loss Drawdown vs. Percent to Recover	
% Loss of Capital	% of Gain Required to Recoup Loss
10%	11.11%
20%	25%
30%	42.85%
40%	66.66%
50%	100%
60%	150%
70%	233%
80%	400%
90%	900%
100%	broke

On the left, the capital lost (in percentage). On the right, what we have to do to get back on par. A gap is evident. The more we lose, the more difficult it will be to recover. It is therefore essential to use a low leverage (in general), especially in salary accounts. As for the small test-accounts, as we said before, dare more, if you have a good strategy that at the moment works well. But if things go wrong right away, the bill is to be thrown away.

Martingale.

Martingale strategies are one of the oldest speculation systems. Its applications to games of chance in addition to financial markets have been the focus of abundant academic studies.

In basic terms, the Martingale strategy suggests that a player takes a default profit on a win and doubles the risk value after a loss. Assuming that the game in question has 50/50 odds with respect to the player, and the player "doubles" always after a loss, a profit is guaranteed because the bigger bets cover the minor losses.

In practice, joining the Martingale requires a great risk. The capital needed to double the value after a series of prolonged losses is substantial. Consider the following scenario assuming a 50/50 probability of success, the net gain is equal to the net loss and the initial risk value is only $ 1. The necessary risk capital after a relatively small number of consecutive losses increases exponentially:

- 5 consecutive losses: US $ 31
- 8 consecutive losses: US $ 479
- 10 consecutive losses: US $ 2.015

As shown in the example, consecutive losses are devastating for the sustainability of the Martingale and can quickly lead to the "ruin of the gambler" .

In the financial world, the Martingale system has been practiced for years. Because the markets are dynamic, the opportunity is present. Provided you use a limited and very light martingale, in key points of the chart that we believe to be effective. The Martingale does not necessarily have to be voted on the doubling of "mail". It can very well increase the "mail" by 30%, perhaps extending the profit target and obtaining the same result.

In theory, adding leverage increases the ability to capitalize on a market reversal (see the book

Hedge Strategies by Mauri Zucchi, or **Hedge Revolution**). In practice, the capital needed to transport large negative positions can be overwhelming, if you do not have statistical information, and on money management.

The advantages of Martingale in trading:

- Some strategies offer greater chances of success.
- Improve the possibility of supporting short-term profitability.

The disadvantages of Martingale in trading:

- The leverage needed to increase exposure can multiply rapidly.

- Black swans can be a problem.

Antimartingale.

We have just seen the martingale, risky systems to turn a loss into a gain (or an even greater loss). We will now see their opposite, the antimartingales. If we consider that a martingale voted to double, before or after burning the bill, we immediately think that if we do the reverse we should earn millions of dollars, right? Let's see how it works.

The antimartingala, being the opposite of the martingale, has many small losses in the face of a more rare event, the gain, which will lead to recover everything with interest. If the martingale (example) doubles the stakes at each unfavorable event, the antimartingale doubles the stakes at each favorable event. Let's summarize everything with an image.

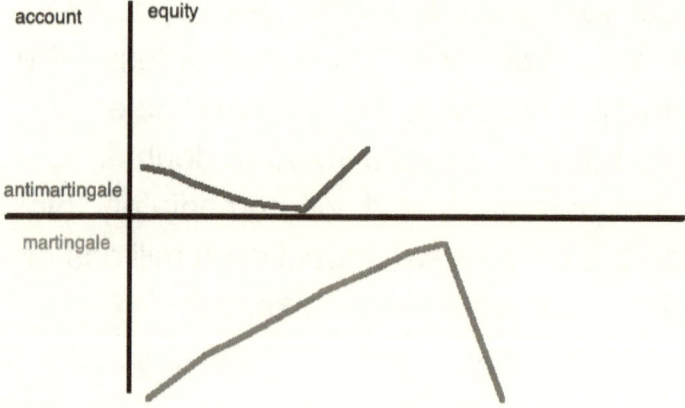

As we can see in the figure above, the antimarting strategy should yield, after so many small losses, a rare favorable event that brings the gain account. The equity of the martingale (green) in theory, instead after so many small gains, meets an unfavorable event that burns the bill.

The antimartingala, therefore, works like this: every time a positive trade is made, the mail is doubled. But what happens when we double the post on positive trades (sequences go well)? It happens that if we take a losing trade, we lose all the gain of several previous trades. This tiring method is obvious that it has limits: we may find ourselves having made 4 trades in gain, and always doubling the post or almost, at the fifth trades we lose. But we do not just lose that trade, we also lose the previous 4. If the martingale, according to the law of large numbers, before or after burning the bill finding a big event favorable (for example, 10-12 negative trades), the antimartingale can instead, for the opposite, find a large exponential gain, in fact after 10-12 positive trades, all voted for doubling of mail. A stellar gain. Now you will say that the antimartingale is therefore the solution to all ills. But I tell you that it is practically the same thing as the martingale, with pros and cons. We explain why.

Psychology. Making 10-12 positive events, all doubling the stakes, is something psychologically difficult. The trader, after 4.5.6 positive trades, is tempted to break the sequence and keep the swag. "All right," you say. No, not good, because if in the martingale you have so many small gains in the face of a big loss, nell'antimartingala we have many losses in the face of a few gains. If we do not go all the way with the few gains that arise, we will be swept away by the many small losses.

Very rare favorable events. Let's also have an iron psychology and go all the way. If, as we have seen, in the martingale you can have favorable periods that can last months / years, in the same way in the antimartingale you could expect years of small losses before guessing "the perfect sequence" that makes us recover all the losses and give us a big gain. This event is rare, and even if we dilute it in a simpler event (with a trading system), it will be increasingly rare for continuous small losses that occur continuously. Are we really sure to be in front of the PC when the event will be presented? What if we were sick? Or on holiday just that day, or by the mechanic ..? Think what it means, wait a month for an event, making small losses every day, and then the right day you have not traded .. It happens, and it happens to many traders. The most sophisticated will then use an EA (expert advisor) that will do the dirty work for them, 24 hours a day. Well, let's just say that it is very difficult for an expert to absorb such a job, especially on intraday, because the pitfalls are always around the corner (slippages, spread widgets, news, price that makes the EA "go crazy" .. (on graphs with stoploss and takeprofit wide is more feasible, but obviously times are lenghty.)

With this we do not want to say that the antimartingale is to be thrown away, on the contrary, it is an excellent method of study to test strategies, but make sense and a right progression, like the martingale.

Kelly formula.

A mathematical formula that arises from the statistical work done years ago. as for the trading and investment, the formula attempts to define the optimal amount of capital to risk of a given trade based on the probability of the success of that trade.

it promotes the idea that an increase in capital risk is justified by a higher probability of success. for example, if an exchange has a probability of success of 95%, then the appropriate amount to be allocated is much greater capital of an exchange with a much lower success rate (5%).

Calculation can be a challenge, so trading platforms and financial software vendors have automated the ability to perform the calculation promptly. There are many variations of the formula, but many traders and investors use this simplified version:

- Kelly% = W - [(1-W) / R]
- W = percentage of winning trades.

- R = Average earning of winning transactions / Average loss of losing trades.

The mechanisms of Kelly's formula for an expected success rate of 70%, a 10% gain and a 10% loss are performed as follows:

- Kelly% = .70 - [(1-.70) / (.1 / .1)] = .40 then 40%.

In this situation, the appropriate risk reaches 40% of the trading account.

Advantages:

- Large potential returns.
- Ability to maximize returns on high-probability transactions.

Disadvantages of the formula:

- Losses lead to disaster.
- The high probability of success is equivalent to enormous risk values.

As we have seen, any defensive art of money management in online trading has pros and cons. The important thing is to study them all, get an idea and always be careful. Never take anything for granted. It is always good to first evaluate all the negative variables, then the positive ones.

Overnight factor in Forex.

In Forex, when you hold an open position until the end of the trading day, you will be paid or charged interest on that position, depending on the underlying interest rates of the couple's two currencies. This can depend on a variety of factors.

Let's take an example.

Let's say that the interest rate of the European Central Bank (ECB) is 5.20% and the Fed's (US) interest rate is 3.5%. Open a short position (Sell) on EURUSD for 1 lot. Here, you are essentially selling 100,000 euros, borrowing at a rate of 5.20%. In the sale of EURUSD, you are buying US dollars, which bear interest at 3.5%. When the interest rate of the country whose currency is being bought is higher than the interest rate of the country where the currency is being sold, the space will be added to your trading account (this may not always be valid, as brokers require often a commission for overnight swaps). If the interest rate is higher in the country where the currency is being sold, as in this example (5.20> 3.5), archiving will be deducted from your account.

Now let's say that the broker charges a further 0.25% for the swap. Add this to the difference in interest rates and get what you need to pay. Below is an example of an overnight table. Every broker, on their site, should have this table to consult to know how much to pay each night. As you can see, they are not negligible expenses (the example has 100.000usd standard lot). For example, if you buy long USD / HKD, you would pay $ 7.12 a day.

If you have several pairs, you must take these expenses into account. Fortunately, not all transactions have negative swaps, many in fact have positive interests. If the currencies are diversified it is advisable to make sure that the "mixture" creates a swap rate that is not very incisive, and sometimes positive on the whole amount. Usually, but not always, a positive trend currency offers a negative swap, while a counter-rate currency offers a negative swap. But it's not always like this.

Instrument	Long (pips)	Short (pips)	Long (USD)	Short (USD)
USD/HKD	2.82	-5.59	3.60	-7.12
USD/HUF	1.75	-2.32	6.27	-8.32
USD/ILS	1.33	-3.59	3.66	-9.90
USD/JPY	0.70	-0.99	6.29	-8.83
USD/MXN	-17.90	11.02	-9.27	5.71
USD/NOK	2.83	-5.46	3.27	-6.30
USD/PLN	-0.15	-2.17	-0.40	-5.73
USD/RON	-0.46	-1.90	-11.03	-45.34
USD/RUB	-110.76	65.67	-16.84	9.99
USD/SEK	6.11	-8.81	6.54	-9.42
USD/SGD	0.10	-0.74	0.72	-5.47

Compounding: The art of increasing the account.

In this chapter we will see how Compounding works, that is the technique to increase an exponential trading account. Compounding, in fact, is also used in other businesses, and has allowed large entrepreneurs, financiers, business-man, to become billionaires. The routes of this specialty are many, but we will focus only on online trading. Compounding is a double-edged sword: we first talked about money management as a discipline to preserve and defend capital. Compounding is instead an offensive weapon, like the attack of a football team.

Definition: Compounding is the adjustment of interest on the current investment.

For example, we have a 10,000usd trading account. After a year we made 10%. Now there are 11.000usd on the bill. The following process will be to make 10% no more on 10.000usd but rather on 11.000usd, and so on. Unlike a salary account, which, as we have seen, takes almost all profits, using compounding we must try to increase the bill at an exponential level, especially when the market is favorable. The advantage is that the risk remains the same: adjusting the trades to the new equity of the account, if we had a 1% risk to trade, will not change. The advantages of this technique are therefore numerous, provided you have an excellent tested trading system, and have experience in the field. In fact, we recommend that you undertake this after a lot of practice on demo accounts. Compounding therefore increases leverage as the bill increases, and decreases as the bill decreases. The days that you do not earn anything, you leave everything unchanged. Those in which you lose are lowered accordingly. Therefore maintaining the same trading profile.

Obviously, each strategy involves different money management, sizes trades, etcetera et cetera. That's your job, first find a good strategy, test and adapt trades and leverage. At that point it is easy to apply a compounding that increases everything as the bill increases, and decreases as the bill decreases.

The table below provides 3 different types of compounding.

type of account	normal	aggressive	very aggressive
months			
1	1000	1000	1000
2	1100	1200	1300
3	1200	1500	1900
4	1350	1800	2900
5	1500	2200	4000
6	1700	2700	6000
7	2000	3400	9000
8	2300	4000	12000
9	2700	4700	16000
10	3100	5700	22000
11	3450	7000	30000
12	3900	9000	45000
compouding every	month	2 weeks	day

The green account, on the left, is a more contained compounding, but always for expert traders. Leverage account adjustment every month (provided there is an increase in the account, of course). The account in the middle is more aggressive, and requires adjustment every two weeks. The third on the right, is very aggressive, exponential, and provides leverage adjustment practically every day (profit). The three accounts are very optimistic, and provide for a long series of days of profit (think of a trend that lasts for 1 year, or a strategy that is giving good steady gains). As you can see, even using a poor 1000usd test bill, you can get amazing results in all three columns. The more experienced traders will obviously be heading towards the more aggressive account, but provided they have a good solid strategy, and money management and statistical math knowledge!

FINAL CONSIDERATIONS.

Money management is the basis of all businesses, whether they are on the street or in front of a PC. An MM serves to protect the business account, to quantify business risks. No business is possible without knowing the risks involved, luck aside. Money management in online trading is as important as in any other business. It is necessary to preserve the account from rare factors but that when they occur they can reset the business account. We need to save on costs (commissions) in the same quality. It is also necessary to have a winning business plan (strategy). And finally, we need to know how much to risk.

We have listed all the possible variables that a successful trader must take into account. We talked about the defensive part, or money management, and the offensive part, or compounding.

To create the best business you need:

Have a business plan, or a tested trading strategy that works.

Identify the costs. A business costs: understanding where and how you can save by always using the same resources.

Prepare money management: understand how much to risk and invest based on the chances of success.

Prepare a possible growth phase: a compounding. It is a non-obligatory phase in all businesses, which involves expanding the company (account) quickly and exponentially, but significantly increasing the risks involved.

In this book we focused on the whole side of the business (or the trading strategy), because before any strategy you need to know how to defend yourself from the pitfalls of the market. In addition to this, it is also possible, with the right experience, to increase the bill in an important way.

www.ingramcontent.com/pod-product-compliance
Lightning Source LLC
Chambersburg PA
CBHW030540220526
45463CB00007B/2914